JILEA HEMMINGS

THE

UNTOLD TRUTH

ABOUT BUILDING A STARTUP

17 LESSONS EVERY ENTREPRENEUR NEEDS TO KNOW

HEMMINGS PUBLISHING

This book is dedicated to my family:
my loving husband, Jamie, my amazing children
Jayden, Jaxon, & Jia.

Contents

Introduction

I wrote this book to tell entrepreneurs the real truth about starting a business. Most books will give you the textbook basics and we will touch on that as well, but the main focus of this book is to share with you the game changing information that most people will never tell you about building your business. When you say you are starting a business people will congratulate you, but the majority will never tell you about the ride you are in for. Do not get me wrong building a business is one of the most thrilling, challenging, tiring, and rewarding things you can do in your life, if you are building the right business. I will discuss choosing the right business to launch in a later chapter.

I have built businesses and graduated from Business School and as I look back and reflect on my experience, I find myself saying if I would of known this I would have made better choices and different decisions.

I will share key lessons I have learned through my journey in building my businesses that you can apply in building yours. The lessons being discussed are applicable no matter what business your starting.

What helped me in my journey of entrepreneurship is never being afraid to fail. You will have to be a fearless leader no matter what the obstacle. Your ideas will seem radical to others, like the Pet Rock or the Snuggie which both sold millions. But it is that type of radical thinking that will set you apart from the rest. On your path to building your business, you will experience failure and make mistakes along the way. What you learn from your mistakes will be vital in building a successful business. I would love to say it will be smooth sailing and you will become a multi-millionaire from your business in the first year, but unfortunately that is not the truth for most new startups. 80% of businesses fail in the first 18 months of operation. You will come across bumps in your path, but it is about learning from your mistakes and pushing through.

Remember, when you learned to ride a bike. Did you just jump on? No, you fell down several times before you learned to balance. The way you learned to ride a bike is the same way you will learn to build your business. But remember your parents held onto to the back of the bike to give you guidance. This is what my book represents.

This book will teach you how to make the right decisions in day to day business operations which will help you reach new levels of success!

Start The Right Business For The Right Reason

"Chase the vision, not the money; the money will end up following you."

—Tony Hsieh, Zappos CEO

There are lots of reasons to start a business and, if you're reading a book with "*The Untold Truth About Building A StartUp*" in the title, you have obviously thought of one.

I know I had many business ideas and the ones that interested me most were the ones where I could make the most money, or at least when I *thought* I could. Before you venture into a new business I ask that you consider this: Don't start a business just because it sounds good. Lots of things in life sound good, like eating three slices of chocolate cake in one sitting! But we all know that eating three slices of cake is not good for your health. The same rule applies in business: just because something *sounds* good doesn't necessarily mean it's going to *be* good for your ultimate success.

Instead, you need to examine other, more relevant reasons for opening your own business, to include your purpose, passion, strengths and talents.

> Your business should reflect your purpose and passion first. Your strengths and your talents will complement your purpose.

I know you might be saying to yourself right now, "Where are you going with this?" Well, simply put, I don't want you to make the same mistakes I did. Which mistakes? All of them, frankly, but first, a little background: I started a business out of desperation and fear.

I was worried about losing my job and knew I needed to have a back up plan. So I decided to kick-start a food entrée line for kids. This idea came out of a personal need for my own kids needing to eat healthy even on their busiest days. I knew most families had the same guilt I had when feeding their kids traditional fast food and I wanted to provide them with a healthier option.

I also felt that it would be extremely lucrative, once parents discovered the solution I was offering. My purpose in pursing my business was great, but did I possess the skillset?

My passion is to create businesses, my strengths and talents are tenacity, creativity, relationship building, and business development. Nowhere in my past experience or in my pool of strengths and talents was being a chef listed, yet I built a business based on cooking.

In fact, I must confess that I didn't even like cooking at all. Most chefs will tell you that cooking is their therapy. My therapy is business creation. Can you see the mistake I made? I like business creation, however I started a food business.

From this mistake I learned two invaluable lessons:

1. Don't start a business because it looks like there is a lot of money to be made.

2. Don't start a business that is not supported by your life's purpose and passion.

After deciding the direction you wish to pursue, it is important to ask yourself two good questions:

- If you received no monetary compensation for your business, would you still do it anyway?

- Does your business energize you even when you're tired?

If the answer to these questions is "no," then **stop immediately.** You do *not* want to start a business that you would not want to do if you receive no compensation whatsoever.

While we all need money to live on, the reality when starting your own business is that you should be prepared to work harder than you ever have for any employer, dedicate more time and make more sacrifices in your life style than you ever dreamed about, especially on a family basis for little to no compensation in the beginning anyway. What will make you continue is your love for what you do.

Money should *not* be the driving force of your purpose and passion. Yes, money will be required to drive your business forward, and keep it alive, but it should not be the primary reason you pursue your business.

**When your purpose and direction marry,
that is the true recipe for success.**

Ultimately, the monetary compensation that comes from that union will be an added perk, but not the basis for getting into business in the first place.

Gut Check Time
Questions for Review

After each chapter, I will provide a few simple "gut check" questions to help solidify what you've just learned, and prepare you for the next step of the journey. Here is your "gut check" for Chapter 1:

- What is your purpose/passion?

- Do you have a business idea already in mind?

- Do you think you have the type of risk tolerance necessary to start your own business?

- Are you ready to learn more?

Don't Spend 1 Penny Without A Plan

"A good plan is like a road map: it shows the final destination and usually the best way to get there."

—H. Stanley Judd

Before you invest a single dollar in your startup, you must create a business plan. You need to have a clear and concise road map of how you are going to execute this great idea. The same is true in life!

You don't get on the road before having specific instructions on how to get where you're going. You don't bake a cake without reading the recipe and you should not build a business without a business plan.

Every business needs an instruction manual – a blueprint, if you will – outlining how it is going to be created and operated.

Investing money without a business plan is an absolute recipe for disaster. However, creating a business plan can be a very time consuming process. In Chapter 14, I discuss understanding your skill sets and outsourcing. In case, you decide to hire someone else to create your business plan, know that your input and tweaking will be extremely important to having an accurate plan.

You may ask yourself what components go into to creating a business plan and how do they fit together? Here is a list of the key sections that go into a well constructed plan:

- Executive summary
- Mission
- Your concept
- Your credibility
- Your industry
- The process
- Market research
- Targets and competition
- About your business

- SWOT
- Personnel
- Potential profit
- Cash flow
- Cash flow assumptions
- Break even
- More actions
- Conclusion

One of the most valuable benefits of the exercise of creating a business plan from the ground up is that it will bring to light the strengths and weaknesses about your company. In essence, this plan will act as a guide to let you know if you are pursuing the right business in the right way or why this idea should not be pursued any further.

Your plan will also reveal how much money you will need to get your business going and also to sustain it.

A good business plan will cover all the things you need to know to improve your chances for developing a successful business structurally and financially.

Overall, a business plan will help to determine if you have a solid enough foundation upon which to proceed. I know this list seems really daunting at the moment, but trust me – there are people to help! In fact, that's what our very next section is about.

Don't Go It Alone

In order to ensure that your business plan is well put together, consider utilizing one or all of the valuable resources below:

- **US Small Business Administration.** The SBA can help you create a business plan. Visit them at **www.sba.gov.**

- **The Small Business Company.** The Small Business Company offers "Interactive tools, diagnostics and engaging content to help your website visitors develop their business plans." Visit them at **www.tsbc.com**

- **SCORE.** SCORE is a "nonprofit association dedicated to helping small businesses get off the ground, grow and achieve their goals through education and mentorship." They have dozens of resources on creating a business plan, from templates to advice and much, much more. Visit them at **www.score.org.**

- **Private Consulting Firms.** Finally, there are dozens of small business consulting companies that can help you, such as our company, Eshe Consulting. Visit us at **www.esheconsulting.com** to learn more!

Your business plan is too important to trust to chance. If you feel like you need help, any or all of the above options could be right for you.

If you're thinking of having someone else create your plan for you, keep in mind that the cost for a professional business plan is about $2,000 to $3,000. It may seem like a lot, but it could be one of the best investments you ever make in your company.

No matter what you do, don't invest a single dollar in pursuing your own business until you know where you're headed first. That means creating a road map, a blueprint or instruction manual. In our case, it means creating a business plan.

Gut Check Time
Questions for Review

- Do you now value the importance of a solid business plan?

- Do you understand what it takes to create your own business plan?

- Do you have the proper resources to know where to find someone to help you create a solid plan for your business?

Personal Guarantee vs. Business Guarantee

> The cardinal rule of business is never to sign a personal guarantee in business. Let's appreciate the fact that a person and business are two different entities.
>
> —B.S. Rao

Do you ever wonder why wealthy people like Donald Trump and Walt Disney are able to file for bankruptcy multiple times yet their personal lifestyle is not affected! Well, that's because they ensure that everything related to their business (agreements, assets, liabilities, etc.) are in the company name.

You may ask why do they do this. The reason behind this important operating decision is that they do not wish to carry any business liability they no longer own. Like them, we all want our businesses to thrive, but let's be real – a lot of businesses fail. According to Bloomberg, 8 out of 10 entrepreneurs who embark on businesses fail within the first 18 months, and a whopping 80% crash. The last thing you want is to have a business closure with an open debt. Let's walk through an example of what this might look like: Assume you just started a new business and need to finance inventory of goods, secure an office location and purchase a vehicle for transportation. Now, you could open a bank account in your name to purchase the inventory, rent an office location and purchase a work vehicle with you as the personal guarantee. This is a great scenario if your business is thriving. But what if you acquired all these liabilities and the sales never take off or slow down significantly? How do you pay your expenses? Well, this detailed case occurs more often than not. When you present yourself as the personal guarantor, all those expenses will be your responsibility – whether your business is running or closed.

Now, on the flip side, if those same liabilities are listed in the company name, then you shall have no personal commitment to pay for those business expenses.

Another good example is that of a company where the founder of an LLC company provided a personal guarantee for the franchise business. The business did extremely well for over a decade, but later the business revenues nosedived. With heavy debts, the founder wished to opt out of the franchise, but the agreement signed with the principal company stated that he would be liable for twenty years with the franchiser.

After reviewing the contract, it was uncovered that the founder personally guaranteed the business even though no collateral was involved. The only way the franchise owner could resolve the issue was by filing a personal Chapter 7 bankruptcy which eliminated the personal liability.

Hence, it is prudent to ensure that all liabilities and purchases are in the company name. And just in case your business (unfortunately) has to close up shop, you can file for business bankruptcy and all your business liabilities are washed away with no future repercussion, unlike personal bankruptcy that stays on your credit for seven years.

If you are reading this chapter and want to kick yourself for listing yourself as the personal guarantor, don't. There is still hope as, in a lot of cases, you can still modify the original agreement, especially if you are in good standing with your the accounts. The most important thing is to review all your contracts and change the liability into your company name and list your company name as the guarantor in all future contracts.

Gut Check Time
Questions for Review

- Are you the personal guarantor for business liabilities?

- Do you thoroughly read all documents and contracts to understand your personal liability, if any?

- Can you amend any contracts or agreements where you listed yourself as a personal guarantor and change it into your company name?

Business Basics

A business that makes nothing but money is a poor business.

—Henry Ford

Now that you have created an airtight business plan, it is important to understand the basics of what it takes to start and operate any organization.

Structure

How and where you setup your business structure (sole proprietorship, llc, c-corp etc) is very important. In a sole proprietorship, the owner and the business are treated as one. This means that the owner of the business has personally agreed to take all of the risks of the enterprise. In other words, the creditors can take legal actions against you and your personal assets if the debt is not paid. As discussed in the last chapter, that you can't be the personal guarantor for your business. I would not recommend your business be setup as a sole proprietorship.

A limited liability company (LLC) takes away the personal liability and you are shielded from the debts and obligations of the LLC. An LLC is a pass-through entity, which means that you are not double taxed like a corporation. You can also file your personal return and your LLC together as well. LLC's are relativity inexpensive to form. When considering bringing on an investor, they may want shares issued. In that case, a corporation will need to be setup because an LLC only allows you to issue a percent of ownership not shares.

A corporation like an LLC does not have personal liability. Corporations issue shares in ownership and that is the extent of the liability. Corporations are double taxed which means that the company income is taxed and the shareholders income is also taxed. Corporations also can be expensive to form and maintain.

Because of the various benefits, or lack thereof, where you choose to setup your business is very important. For instance, do the laws of your state – or a neighboring one – favor small business more than the other? If you choose to incorporate your company in your home state, that is called a **home state incorporation**. Regardless of the type of business structure you choose, such as an LLC or a C-corporation, each state has its own structure of fees and regulations to which you will have to adhere. This should be one of the main considerations you entertain when choosing which state to incorporate your business entity.

Naming Your Business

Company names without clear pronunci-
ation or spelling won't last.

—David Rusenko

Naming your business is an auspicious next step, and not one to be taken lightly. Before you incorporate your business make sure the name you selected is available in the state where you want to incorporate. Once you see the name is not taken, check to make sure that domain address is available. Once the domain address (URL) is available. Begin to formal-ize your structure in the following order. First, incorporate the structure in the state you choose and wait for approval from the state.

The state might ask you to change the name of your busi-ness if it is too close to another entity name, so please do not move on to the next step before receiving verification from the state. Once your incorporation has been verified, then and only then should you purchase the domain name.

You want to purchase all the extensions available, for in-stance .com, .org, .biz. .co., so that you do not have to wor-ry about another organization purchasing a website close to yours and your customers having the possibility of getting confused when searching for your business.

Corporate Identity

Now that you have decided on a structure. Location, and name it is time to create the corporate identity for your business. Your corporate identity is your organization's brand. It is important that your logo, stationary, business cards, brochures and website all look like they are part of the same family. After all, this is your customer's first introduction to your business and it needs to be clear, concise and professional.

The reason I was able to sit at the table with big organizations was because they felt that our corporate identity and product branding was so professional we must be a big organization and not a two person show. Why did they insinuate that from our corporate identity and product branding? Think of it like this, when you get your hair done do you want a hairdresser whose hair is a mess or one whose hair looks good? You want the hairdresser who hairs looks good because you assume they will be able to make your hair look good. Another example is a kid who comes to class wrinkled with his homework all crumpled up and a kid who comes with their clothes ironed and their homework organized. One kid seems more serious, had more respect for themselves, and paid more attention to the details. The same rules apply in business. First impressions matter and if you put the time and detail into how your corporate identity and branding looks you will put the same detail into the product or service you will deliver to the client.

Now it is time to create a logo, a symbol that represents your brand. This logo should be the design statement for the whole company. The rest of the branding for the organization should use the logo as a guide for the style of every branding piece created. It is important that your logo is legible and applicable to what your business is all about. I would opt out of a tremendous amount of colors due to the increased cost this will represent when it comes time to purchasing promotional items for your business such as shirts, mugs, etc. When it comes to design, more colors = more cost.

Once you are happy with the logo, then it is time to trademark the logo. This is so that no one else takes it. Whoever files the trademark first usually gets to keep it. Unless you can show years of it being utilized heavily before the new entity filed their trademark. The legal fees to prove this are enormous. So let's be safe and insure that it is registered.

Once your logo is trademarked, you now need to think about product, brand, and service offering and design a website to reflect that vision. As I mentioned earlier, you always want to look like a major entity in how you present your company. It makes it look like you care.

This does not have to cost a fortune. You can find students in graphic design school that would welcome a project like this to beef up their portfolio.

There are several hundred freelancers available online that are well versed in creating brands. Always ask for samples of their previous work before hiring them. Which brings me to another important point: every person that helps you with your business needs to sign a non-disclosure agreement (NDA).

This document insures that your information, ideas or anything else related to your company cannot be shared or replicated. If this agreement is not signed then they can replicate your organization and if they have more resources and connections than you, can actually beat you to the punch. They can hit shelves or offer the exact same service to the same clientele you were pitching. We will discuss trust in business in a later chapter.

Product/Service Offering

In your business plan, hopefully you have laid out what products and services you will offer. You need to offer something that is better and different than your competition so that you will differentiate yourself in the marketplace. I mentioned earlier that one of the reasons we were allowed to sit at the table with big organizations was that our company looked the part and the second reason is that we brought something different to the table, something very unique.

We were the first to manufacture frozen entries for kids based on traditional kids' favorites with a meatless substitute as the protein source. If we had presented a "me too" product I guarantee you that we would have not made any traction. Now there is Burger King *and* McDonalds, so there is always room for competition in the same genre, but there

J I L E A   H E M M I N G S

is a difference between the two entities that is distinct. In other words, you want to stand out. Also, if you cannot offer a product or service consistently, do not offer it. The worst thing a customer can hear is "we are all out," or "we are not offering that service today."

This does not mean that you don't offer specials, but if you cannot meet the demands of your customer consistently, they will take their business elsewhere. This will result in a missed opportunities and, in business terms, lost sales. It is imperative that the product be unique and address the unmet needs of consumers. This will ensure it's commercial success.

Marketing & Promotion

There are great brands and products that exist in the marketplace that no one knows about and I would venture to say ever will, strictly because they do not understand the importance of proper marketing. Marketing your business properly is extremely important to your company having staying power. There are tons of horrible products on the market right now that have great marketing. I am sure your tried your share of them. The disappointment stems from you not getting what the box promised. So you ask yourself why are they still on the market. One answer **Great Marketing**. One of my professors used to say that it doesn't matter whats in the box what matters is what's on the box. I will take the lesson one step further to say, as a small company you need great marketing and superior products and services to have a shot in surviving at all. The big boys can have great marketing and a crappy product because they have brand recognition and a large enough product offering of which all their products are not crap. As a new entrant you need to make sure your marketing is flawless. This is what most marketing agencies know and that is the recipe of how to build customer loyalty.

Brand Awareness is key to having success with your brand and service offering. Studies have shown that people need to see your brand 7 times before they will purchase it once. This is why you want your marketing to be clear and be memorable.

How you promote your brand is also important. You need to make sure that your marketing is directed at the right target market. If you have the best product but your targeting your marketing to the wrong audience you are doomed. I learned this the hard way. We spent money on PR companies, commercials, gorilla marketing, etc.. We were aiming at trying to reach anyone. What we received in return was very few quality customer leads. You truly need to understand who your customer is, what they want, and how they like to get it. All of your marketing needs to be centered around your target market, those who understand what your product or service is and actively seek out what your offering on their own. You do not want to start with a cold market that will require a lot of education to understand the value of what you are offering.

Social media is becoming the most effective way to market to your potential customers. It is no longer an optional tool. It does not have to be very costly, as now you can reach your targeted consumer based on inputting certain criteria and decide how much you are willing to pay to get the desired customer lead. What is great about online marketing is you set your own budget. When the budget is used its used until you decide that marketing effort was worth reinvesting in. Our marketing was not 100% directed at our targeted consumer and did not have a long shelf life. TV is one media choice that unless you have an endless budget of cash or great brand recognition will die off very quickly. Once the commercial or the segment goes off the air how will target market see it again? You can record it for your website and your media kit and sometimes networks might replay segments. The most important thing to know is what each marketing medium part plays in your overall marketing plan. For example, your company is featured on a major network TV show like the Today show. Your goal is to increase your national credibility which can be used in your media kit and/or your website to show you are a real company with positive reviews. Another example, is you want readers on a popular healthy living blog to know that you offer health conscious meals solutions on the go. Through having a blogger write a review on your service now someone who your target market associates with providing credible advice is endorsing your brand. There are many different marketing strategies that can fit well together as long as you understand your target market and insure they will be touched everytime you market your brand.

Financial Management

No business in the world has ever made
more money with poor management.

—Bill Terry

It is important to setup proper financial management. What do I mean by this? I mean that you need to establish a separate bank account from your personal account right away. You will need get a EIN number from the IRS.gov site. Your organization's EIN number is like a business social security number. It is used to identify and track your organization's transactions and credit worthiness.

It will be extremely important that you pay your expenses on time. Which brings me to my next point: you need to track your expenses. There are plenty of financial management systems available to help. I like Quick Books personally. They offer the ability for you to manage your business transactions online, which is a great feature because they are always backed up. If you've ever had your whole system crash and lost all your information, then you understand the value of an online backup.

You need to input your business transactions on a daily basis. Why? Because it is very easy to get behind on recording your transactions and create a nightmare for yourself. What nightmare? When someone asks you to produce a statement of health on your organization to qualify for something that your organizations needs and you have to input all your business transactions at one time, which can be a daunting task.

You always need to know how much your company has earned in a given year and whether you are making a profit or loss – and by how much. A lot of people will outsource this task if they do not know how to manage and track finances. There are, in fact, many businesses that specialize in doing just that. The most important aspect to financial management is to develop a system and keep it up to date.

Insurance

Proper insurance coverage is extremely important to have on your business. Each industry has requirements on the levels of insurance you company needs to carry. A lot of businesses do not understand the importance of carrying liability insurance and sometimes opt out if it is not mandated. What if a customer has a bad outcome to a product ordered or service delivered and decides to pursue legal action? If you have insurance, then you are protected with the only financial repercussion being an increased policy premium. If you do not have insurance, you can lose your entire business, especially if you have to sell it to pay damages to the victim. I hate to present doom and gloom before you've even started your company, but reality is reality. I would not want all the hard work and investment you have dedicated to build your business be lost because your business was not properly covered.

A 2009 study in United States found that a lack of insurance contributes to the deaths of over 45,000 Americans each year. Now, can you imagine running a business without insurance?

Operational Management

Moving forward, the day to day operations will consume a lot of your time. In the beginning, to conserve costs, you will have to manage every aspect of the business. Those aspects include: employees, expense management, supply management, sales, marketing, etc. It can be quite an arduous task, but you can outsource aspects of the business that are out of your realm of expertise. Outsourcing can become costly, but we will discuss outsourcing in more detail in a later chapter. An important thing to note is that, in that list above, I did not mention your specific niche or business idea. The tasks listed above are just the basic operational needs that will need to be managed on top of your specific business needs. As an employee, you only have to manage a specific task or role. Being a business owner means you have to manage every aspect of what it will take to make your business run and be successful.

The rest of the book will give you tips on how to manage you business and key aspects that you need to know through all the phases of getting your business up and running.

Gut Check Time
Questions for Review

- What type of business structure are you going to setup and in what state?

- Do you have a company logo and if you do, is it trade-marked?

- What is your product or service offering?

- Have you setup a plan to handle managing business financing?

- Do you have proper insurance coverage?

- Who is going to run the daily business operations?

Beware of Putting All Your Eggs in One Basket

"Do not put all your eggs in one basket."

—Warren Buffett

If you plan for your business to be your sole stream of income, think again. The goal for your business is to generate a significant profit and recoup your investment. But it is imperative for you to think of your business as one stream of income – not as the only stream of income.

The fact is, one business is rarely enough to fulfill all your financial needs these days, so you need to have several streams of income to ensure that your overall financial outlook is healthy. And while it's tempting to put all our eggs in one basket, financially speaking, those multiple streams should be spread out over several "baskets". For instance:

- One stream in business,

- One stream in property rentals,

- One stream in the stock market ...

I could go on and on, but I think you get the general idea. In short, your business needs to be your focus, but not your only focus. Use the principles you learn while operating this business to help find success in your other streams of income. For instance, learning to negotiate contracts in your "primary" business can help negotiate better deals when investing in real estate for example.

Every business is a gamble, and not all gambles pay off. Case in point: sometimes we place a bet on only one horse but, if we really want to "hedge" our bet and ensure that we get something back on our investment, we need to spread our bet across more than one horse. This is important so we do not become too dependent on one horse's outcome.

You make better decisions when it's not all or nothing, with everything on the line. Sure, it's "sexier" to imagine ourselves hitting the big payoff by betting on one horse – or, in our case, one business-slash-income stream – but that kind of "all or nothing" thinking tends to lead to desperation when our bets aren't paying off and we still have the rent to pay and vendor bills piling up.

Unfortunately, I learned this lesson the hard way! Once upon a time, I thought my business was going to provide financial freedom for me and my family. Over time, I systematically cashed out my 401K and my spouse and I began to use bigger and bigger percentages of our salaries to keep our sole business going. This went on to the point that I depleted all my assets because I felt our business was going to be successful. We bet on only one horse and, unfortunately, we lost the bet.

WARNING: Don't do that!

I'm a firm believer in separating personal funds from professional funds, but I know that isn't always feasible for new business owners.

If personal funds *are* going to be involved as "operating capital" for your business, at least set a firm, reasonable limit on how much and from where you are going to draw the funds.

For instance, if you have $10,000 in a savings account, $5,000 in an IRA account and $20,000 in your 401K, only consider taking money from your savings account. The IRA and 401K come with heavy tax penalties for removing funds before retirement. I would also not look to deplete your savings either. You need to always have money in the bank for a rainy day. Whatever amount you decide to invest from your savings needs to be replaced once the business – or businesses – begin to perform and profit.

If you get into the habit of depending too much on your personal accounts to bail out your business, you'll never be fully motivated to make the business self-sustaining. Like a kid with an allowance, you'll always be standing there in front of your personal accounts as a hand out, looking for a quick bail out if you do not set a limit!

Whatever you do, don't start a business from money put aside for retirement. That is a recipe for disaster, plain and simple. That's why identifying accounts that are less critical, like your savings account, helps keep you away from "no touch" accounts that could affect your quality of life in your golden years, like your retirement funds, or even the equity in your home.

Look, no one starts a business thinking it is going to fail. Why would anyone do that? The reality is, however, that most businesses *do* fail. So going in, the odds are already stacked against you. Do you *really* want to compound those bad odds by putting all your eggs into one basket – or all your bets on a single horse?

We live in a fantasy world, a world of illusion. The great task in life is to find reality.

—Iris Murdoch

I don't say this to scare you. I say this to make you aware of the difference between reality and fantasy, between how you think business will be and how it really is. We planned for a fairytale story of business success and, by ignoring the harsh reality, we ended up losing our home and our retirement funds in the process.

It's not easy to admit that kind of failure, but I say this because I would *never* want anyone to have to experience what my family and I have been through due to fairytale plans in a very competitive, very challenging *real* world.

So, learn this lesson: You need to plan how much you are going to invest to give this new business venture a chance.

Have a set limit and stick to it, no matter how tempting it is to tap into whatever funds you have available to make a go of it.

Keep your eyes open and go into any business venture knowing that it should not be your sole revenue stream. Instead, have one, two, or three more going – across multiple industries – to ensure that if something happens to one, you still have plenty of other eggs in your basket to ensure a nice, fluffy omelet at the end of the day!

Gut Check Time
Questions for Review

- Do you have your heart set on starting this business, no matter what?

- Have you put too many eggs in one basket?

- Are you willing to concede defeat if it doesn't work out?

- What are some potential other income streams you might consider if "Plan A" doesn't work out?

Build a Dream Team to Ensure Success

A team is a key component of every business. A 'Good Team' shall ensure business success.

—B.S. Rao

Having the right team is critical to the success and future of your new business venture. We must all stand on our own two feet when it comes to starting a business, but that in no way means you should go at it alone.

Before you start your business, you need to build a team of support to help you reach your long-term goals.

This team is your "go to" squad of A-list players, specifically chosen to help you succeed, regardless of the industry or sector you ultimately choose to play in.

This elite team will act as your "sounding board" for your most important business decisions, and be the calm, rational voice you need to hear when emotions flare or when you can't trust yourself to think straight. Why do you ask? Because they are removed from the emotional ups and downs that you will be faced with when handling the challenges that arise for any business owner.

So, who should be on this "dream team"? There are four key groups of people you will want in your dream team:

Business Partners

Your business partners and investors should be the first people in your team.

It is important that all decisions made about the company be made together, with all owners in the business entity present and accounted for. This will ensure that you are all on the same page and that everyone on the team is operating from the same "playbook".

Financial Advisor(s)

Your accountant is an extremely important member of your team, preferably a qualified Certified Public Accountant. H&R Block© and/or Turbo Tax© just won't do.

When making important financial decisions, it's important to have a CPA advise you on the best ways to operate financially.

The local H&R Block© and Turbo Tax© office is simply for processing tax returns. They're not meant to provide financial advice on how to structure and develop your business objectives to determine whether they are advantageous or not.

A Legal Eagle

In these litigious times, you'll also need a legal expert for contracts, negotiations, conflict resolution and to handle any perceived – or real – legal threats.

A qualified business attorney can also help you draw up contracts and offer both short- and long-term legal advice to help you grow your business.

Another Entrepreneur(s)

Finally, and most importantly, your team should also include trusted business advisors, preferably other entrepreneurs who have already done what you are trying to do. These advisors – commonly referred to as mentors – can help you avoid problems they've already encountered, or offer advice to help you try new methods you never thought possible.

In this case, random generic entrepreneurs won't do. You need to specifically seek out advisors/mentors who have operated in the same space you are entering. They will have a tremendous amount of wisdom and are usually more than happy to share their experience and provide advice. They will often even do it for free, especially if they believe in what you are doing on a personal and professional level. It is wise to surround yourself with people who are like minded.

You might be asking how to go about finding these mentors. Here are some of the best places to find mentors:

- Business owners who are operating similar businesses. Now, you may not want to approach direct competitors, obviously, but try to find a mentor in the same space. For example, I owned a frozen kids entrée line and wanted it to be available in grocery stores. Naturally, I started by looking for a mentor who was making frozen adult meals or at least selling in retail stores. This helped me find advice where I needed it most, with someone who was aware of – and experienced in – my entrepreneurial space.

- Don't reinvent the wheel. Go where like-minded people gather. For instance, organizations like the SBA, Minority Business Supplier Council and Women Certified Business if applicable will be able to set you up with mentors without you having to necessarily do all the legwork from scratch. Time is valuable, so if you can make use of resources that are already set up and available, why wouldn't you?

- Finally, look for mentors outside your line of work that you can call on and gain advice, including a lawyer, accountant, business managers, etc. There will always be an issue, question or concern that comes up and having a trusted mentor will expand your options and give you a person to call when they arise.

If you want to be an entrepreneur, it's not a job, it's a lifestyle. It defines you. Forget about vacations, about going home at 6 pm - last thing at night you'll send emails, first thing in the morning you'll read emails, and you'll wake up in the middle of the night. But it's hugely rewarding as you're fulfilling something for yourself.

—Niklas Zennstrom

Remember, entrepreneurship is a very different arena from being an employee. You do not get to check in at 8 a.m. and check out at 5 p.m. This is a 24 hour gig, 7 days a week. It can be extremely taxing at times and is something that you can't really understand until you go through it for yourself.

On the tough days – and there will be tough days, believe me – it's always good to call up those people who've been where you are and have a chat with them.

After all, there is no better person to motivate you – and "gut check" you – than those that understand the game just like you but are not as close to your baby as you are.

Finding mentors and advisors who can be objective when you are subjective and rational when you're emotional will help you make smarter, wiser, less rash decisions than if you were left to your own devices.

Gut Check Time
Questions for Review

- Do you have people in mind for who might be on your team?

- Have you actively started assembling your own "dream team"?

Trust No One Until It Is In Writing (And Not Even Then!)

I think it's important to have some documentation of the past.

—Henry Rollins

When it comes to business, particularly your *own* business, you must start to think like a skeptic. Remember if it sounds too good to be true it probably is!

I know it sounds harsh but developing this mindset now, rather than later, is going to save you a ton of heartache further on down the line. It's a bitter pill to swallow, but the fact is, business is about money, plain and simple.

No matter how many promises potential investors make when their money is on the line, it all comes down to who can provide the biggest bang for their buck! Investors are always shopping for a good investment. Never think that you are the only investment they are considering, and vice versa. The investor should not feel as though they are your only option for gaining investment, even if they are.

> You always need to represent your business from a place of strength, not weakness.

Just because they have a lot of money does not mean a potential investor knows more than you or should direct how your company should be managed. All they have is money. But look at what you have: you have invested your blood, sweat, and tears and you know your business and your target market inside out.

Compare the investor mindset to buying a car. Usually, you test drive several cars and visit several dealerships before you commit to just one. You probably never tell the dealership that you have no interest in their car because they will keep you there longer and try to change your mind.

Instead you say, "I'll be back," even if you have no intention of returning. The exact same concept applies when dealing with investors. They "test drive" a lot of other investments and in the end they might purchase your car, someone else's car, or no car at all.

> The fact is, no one – and I do mean no one – has your best interest at heart. Look out-the bigger the build up-the harder the fall. BEWARE

That is, unless you are going into business with your parents – and even *then* you have to be very careful.

Words are cheap, and actions are valuable. Trust is a commodity few can afford these days. People make so many promises to you, and then they never follow through.

I have sat in front of some of the richest people, seeking an investment, they went through the motions making me feel as though they were interested. They always expressed their interest, asked for additional analysis, which of course takes time and money to produce when in the end they were often never interested in the first place.

Why would they do this? Well, there are three basic reasons why:

1. Maybe they don't want you to spend more time convincing them of something they have already decided they are not going to buy.

2. It could be that they don't want to close the door in case they do not find a better investment;

3. Or, finally, maybe they are just too "chicken" to admit that they are not interested from the start.

It sounds crazy, I know, but that's how people are. They fill your head with dreams rather than tell the truth.

Gut Check Time
Questions for Review

- Do you consider yourself someone who "trusts" too much?

- Or too easily?

- Are you willing to "toughen up" and let people earn your respect, rather than merely giving it away, sight unseen?

Lesson 8

The Truth About Raising Money for Your Business

Funds are lifeline for a Business.

—B.S. Rao

You have this great idea for a business. Now you need to fund it. Where do you start? Your own bank accounts and investments, right?

Wrong! Like most entrepreneurs, my spouse and I first looked at our own resources as the easiest method of "raising funds" to start our own business. Almost immediately, we began the first deadly mistake of finding capital for our business: we started by funding the needs of the business through our paychecks and savings.

When we found that we needed more money to keep our struggling business afloat, we made our second deadly mistake: we went straight to our retirement accounts and wiped them clean.

We all want to retire someday, and tapping into your retirement nest egg is a terrible mistake because not only do you wipe out your retirement investment, but you rob yourself of your own future in the process.

If that's not bad enough, you are paying steep penalties in taxes for withdrawing the money early. When you get to that point of desperation, in all likelihood that is probably the last asset you personally have.

So now, you have to go to the bank to see what might be done, but you've already wiped out your assets, which could have been used for collateral because, now that you're officially broke, you need a loan.

If you have great credit, (which we didn't at the time), you can probably go and seek an SBA loan. Since that was not an option for us, we went to our family.

This is an okay option if your family has significant resources and giving you an investment will not jeopardize their financial well being. Make sure you include a plan once you start to generate profits to pay them back.

For us, we took money from our family and, unfortunately, it was money they needed to retire on soon. Why? We were so confident in our success as most entrepreneurs are. Our products were on the shelves of several grocery stores including Whole Foods & Safeway. We felt that as long as we had capital their was no stopping us. So the risk of our families retirements as well as our own made sense. We told them it was "a smart bet" and "worth the risk".

This was and usually is a horrible mistake because if your business tanks, it becomes next to impossible to pay them back because, by this point, you have already wiped out your personal assets that you could have leveraged to pay them back.

Now, I want to discuss borrowing from friends. It might seem like a less hazardous situation than borrowing from love ones, but quite the opposite is true. In fact, I actually believe that borrowing from friends is worse than borrowing from family.

Here's why: For you to even go to a friend for money, clearly they have to be really close to you. In many ways, they are probably closer than family. You have shared many good memories and they are probably your kids' god parents, or some equivalent thereof. In short, they have never steered you wrong in the past and, instead, have always had your back. Of course they're going to want to help you in any way they can, financially or otherwise!

But now, let's walk through a scenario where you ask a "friend" for money. By this point, you have used all your personal assets, your family assets, and now you're on to your dearest friends.

Naturally, they lend you all they can, as fast as they can, with more promises from you about what a "great" deal it is and how they "can't lose".

So, what happens when your business *doesn't* perform as planned? Your friends probably out thousands, possibly even tens of thousands, of dollars? Forget how badly *you* feel. How do you think they're going to feel or, a more serious question, act?

Your family might let it go because, no matter what, you are family. But friendships can go south very quickly and, even if they don't, you will have a tremendous amount of guilt on your hands because not only did they trust you, but now you don't know how you are going to repay them.

The latter happened to me. I have a really great friend who believed in my business and what I was trying to accomplish. She saw how hard I was working and, like me, figured that hard work had to pay off sometime, right?

So she gave me the money I needed to continue moving forward. But before long our business was in the tank and I still needed to repay the loan. The problem is... there is no business – i.e. income – to pay the loan back.

Now what? Suddenly, you are looking for any means possible to get the money and even making emotional, hasty or even just plain *bad* business decisions to fulfill an obligation to your close friend.

This is a vicious cycle you want to avoid at all costs. It can ruin family relationships, destroy friendships and send you into a spiral of anxiety and grief that will only add insult to injury if, and when, your business folds.

So, if you shouldn't borrow from your own retirement funds, or from family and friends, who/where should you borrow from?

Do it the old-fashioned way. When you have an idea to start a business, write a business plan as we discussed in Chapter 2. This plan puts in writing practical steps you'll take to see your business succeed.

You may also find that you're a good fit for the relatively new financing option of "crowd funding," where you literally ask a few to several to hundred individuals for smaller amounts of money to reach your goals. Visit sites like www.kickstarter.com and www.indiegogo.com to learn more about this exciting opportunity. In exchange for the funds you give rewards based on the level of financial contribution. That is where your liability ends.

With friends and family, the guilt and debt lives on until you are able to pay them back through other means. Trust me, it is an awful feeling and one, I would not want anyone to experience.

I know that most books on this subject would tell you to start with family and friends, but I personally think that's a "no-no" if you value your relationship with them because it will be strained either by the pressure they put on you or your own personal guilt if you are not able to repay them.

One way to avoid getting into the debt spiral, with friends, family or anyone else for that matter, is to keep your personal finances in order.

More than likely, to get your business up and running, you will need to seek capital investment. As part of the loan/investment process, the lender/investor will most certainly look at your personal history. Not surprisingly, if your financial history looks bleak, then your prospects for getting financing will also be bleak as well.

Let me explain what "bleak" looks like, from a financial perspective: delinquent accounts, late payments, not keeping good records, being unable to answer simple basic financial questions… all of these will hurt your ability to get a loan.

So it is extremely important to remember the standard money principles when starting a business. For instance:

- Don't promise or commit to anything you don't legitimately have the money for.

- Don't leverage the money you set aside to pay for rent/mortgage, car payments, the light bill etc… to make your business be successful.

- Don't rack up debt on a credit card just to make your business successful.

- Don't "gamble" with other people's money!

When starting, running or even growing a business, there *will* come a time when you will need to borrow from a bank. If you "borrow from Peter to pay Paul," those same tactics that you used to stay afloat for the time being are the same tactics that are going to bite you in the butt when the bank considers you a "bad" risk.

Debt is never good, but even banks know it is often necessary to start – and run – a business in today's competitive climate. Don't be afraid of borrowing money; be afraid of borrowing it the "wrong" way – and even from the "wrong" people!

Gut Check Time
Questions for Review

- Are your personal finances in order? Have you considered how you are going to fund your company?

- Do you have an action plan for securing financing? Is it spread out over multiple channels?

- Or are you putting all your eggs in one basket?

Failure is the Greatest Teacher

Failures are finger posts on the road to achievement."

—C.S. Lewis

You learn nothing from success except that it feels good. You only learn from failure. The trick to this one is, no one wants to fail. I don't think anyone wakes up in the morning and says, "What a beautiful day! Let's see… how am I going to fail today?!?"

But failure is an inevitable and, I contend, valuable part of owning a business and part of life. Anyone who has a business and says they have not experienced failure is a liar. Maybe they just don't know they've failed or what they've learned from it, maybe they're afraid to admit defeat but, whatever the reason, every business that's still in business has failed at some point.

I have met business owners who are successful, who have said they have never failed, that they have *always* been successful. Now, not only are they lying but the minute I hear them say something like that, I never trust another word they say. If you can't admit defeat, you'll never benefit from learning from failure – and if you can't do that, you don't have anything to say to me.

I wish failure was not life's best teacher, but it is. You will fail at big things, at little things, at important things, and at insignificant things; it is simply the cost of doing business.

My intent in writing this book is to lessen the amount of failure you have to experience, but also to remind you that you *will* experience failure – and that is not something to be afraid of.

Society has made failure out to be an awful thing. When I started my business, my whole focus – especially after leveraging my home, retirement accounts, salaries, friends' and family's money – was fear of failure. What am I going to do? How am I going to make the money back if this does not work to pay everyone back and restore everything I spent? How am I and my family going to survive? The questions, anxiety and uncertainty were driving me insane!

I finally confided in my mentor about how scared I was to fail and he gave me great advice. He said, "What does failure in your business look like? Imagine your business is over and you have lost everything, now what?"

I told him the picture looked pretty grim! He said, "Okay, well, you will get a job again, have to work on paying people back over time and discover something else to get passionate about, but this time you won't make the same mistakes."

He also emphasized that I was more than capable of starting over and creating success again. The most important thing he said to me was, "Now that you understand what failure looks like, get back to winning. If you fail at something and never try again, that is true failure. Most successful people we admire today failed several times before they had their big break. It is about getting back on the saddle and not giving up on yourself."

So many people make failure out to be a bad thing, but it wasn't always that way? Remember when we were kids and failing simply meant falling down and getting back up again?

But this notion that "failure is bad" comes from without. It starts from when we are young when your parents, teachers, and coaches tells you no one wants to be a failure. Get good grades, never miss a day of school, graduate, go to college and be a success. Nobody likes a failure!

As you get older, that same song plays in the back of your mind, over and over again, until it becomes the soundtrack for your life: don't fail, never fail, failing is bad, etc.

Well, we need a new song written because failure is *not* a bad thing. As a matter of fact, when it comes to being an entrepreneur, failure is part of the process, a badge of honor, a sign of individuality and, for a large number of reasons, it is often a "good" thing.

Failure represents courage, leadership and a winning spirit.

The outcome of risk is often failure; that's why it's called a "risk" in the first place. With nothing to risk, you have nothing to gain – and no way to fail.

You have to be extremely courageous to take risks. There are people in this world who take little to no risk. They are so afraid of failing that they never put themselves in its path. They are truly failing because they never see the upside of failure – which is success. What if they didn't fail? What if they succeeded? What might their life look like then?

Instead of asking themselves these very important, very real questions, they focus solely on the negative and let that stop them in their tracks. Failure represents leadership because it takes a leader to go down the road less traveled. For example, it takes a visionary to take what others see as trash and turn it into a successful eco-friendly line of products. It will take creative vision, courage, and a willingness to take risks to bring your vision to life.

"A ship is always safe at the shore – but that is NOT what it is built for."

—Albert Einstein

If you are taking risks, then you are striving to win. You are not taking the risk to lose. When you strive to win, you unlock your creative juices and start uncovering innovative ways to accomplish your goals. This is the sweet spot, the gum in the center of the lollipop, that we are all hoping to taste when we start something new.

Now when it comes to failure, you want to fail on a smaller scale than on a larger scale. Why? Because you will have a better chance at recovering. Rather than risk it all on one big gamble, you want to take calculated risks. If you take a risk that doesn't work out as planned, analyze what you learned from that failed experience so that you do not make the same mistake twice.

In closing, remember that when it comes to business, failure is an option – and one that often teaches you how to succeed.

Gut Check Time
Questions for Review

- Have you ever thought of failure in a positive light before?

- Have you considered times in the past when you've learned from failure?

- How have your past failures made you stronger?

The Power of Relationships

Relationships are the hallmark of the mature person.

—Brian Tracy

Relationships are everything in life – and in business. No matter how good you are, or how well you think you can do it on your own, the right relationships will trump experience and smarts any day.

Think about it: how many times have you seen people who were less qualified, not as educated as you get the position you were most qualified for? I know that it has happened to me plenty of times.

In my professional career, I would take on more projects, stay late, pick up the slack and generally over achieve.

I thought I was going to get ahead because my supervisors and managers would eventually see the good job I was doing and reward me with the promotion I deserved.

Turns out I was busy fulfilling the life long assignment my parents instilled in me from the beginning. Study hard, be the first to come to work and the last to leave. Produce excellent work. Keep your head down, stick it out and, eventually, you will get your just reward.

Do any of these statements resonate with you? Do they sound familiar? Sure they do. We were all taught, growing up, that hard work equals success.

The big piece missing from that equation was that people like working with people they can trust and have relationships with. I hate to say it, but people buy from – and hire people – they like. Not people who show how smart they are or even necessarily work harder than others. It's a hard lesson to learn, especially because it goes against literally everything we were taught as children. How could all those teachers, counselors and advisors be wrong? A better question to ask yourself is, how fast can you unlearn what they taught you and discover the power of relationships for yourself?

To start, you have to find out where the people you do business with spend their time professionally. In the frozen food business the people I needed to interact with all came to this frozen food convention twice a year. They would socialize and conduct business there and it was a place I needed to be if I wanted to build those strategic relationships to help propel my business forward.

In those situations, it was not my hard work or "smarts" that set me apart, but the fact that I was where they were, making an effort, socializing, interacting and networking that made all the difference.

Furthermore, not all relationships are created equal when it comes to networking and support. If you are looking at your immediate support system of family and friends to carry you past the "taste this" phase of your new business, you are setting yourself up for failure. Your best friend can tell three of their friends and your family can follow suit, but it is going to take more than that to make your business successful.

You should start by looking to join organizations in your local area. Join the Chamber of Commerce; they have month-ly meetings where you can meet other entrepreneurs and a platform to introduce your business to other chamber mem-bers who might be able to help propel your business or who need the products and services you offer. Never forget that relationships are a two way street and helping others helps yourself.

The membership fees for most Chambers are nominal, between $25 and $50 per year, and are invaluable to your business. They believe in supporting local business, that is their mandate.

Other organizations to consider include the Minority Business Council, women certified own businesses, business incubators, and the list goes on. Add to it!

> **If you feel there is someone you can, and should, connect with, connect with them!**

For example: If you sell a product that schools would like and you have kids in school and you are *not* a part of the PTA or visiting mommy groups, you are missing your market.

Likewise, if you have a business that caters to athletes and you are not participating in, or sponsoring, or even attending a variety of local athletic events such as softball, soccer and baseball games, you are missing out on important relationships that could take your company to the next level.

Building strategic relationships can be the deciding factor between being in business three years from now or not. Is that something you want to risk just because you feel like hard work and smarts are enough to succeed?

Gut Check Time
Questions for Review

- Who are the most valuable people in your professional network right now?

- Have you considered calling on them to aid you in your quest for starting a company? Who do you think you can add to your list to help you expand your network?

- What is the best way to get a hold of them?

- How soon can you start?

Becoming a Spy

Competitive Intelligence is a key discipline of every business. It's Oxygen for all living businesses.

—B.S. Rao

Just like relationships are a critical factor in determining success, so is your power of observation. In other words, you need to be not only aware of your competition, but actively invest in how they are succeeding – and why.

You need to spend a tremendous amount of time spying on your competition before you invest one dollar in starting your own company.

After that, you will need to continue to spy as long as you are in business.

This is a critical step that you need to understand:

- Why they started their business? Who is their customer base?

- What products do they offer and why?

- Who makes their products?

- If they are profitable or not and why?

- Etc.

But don't stop there. You need to understand and visit their facility. How big is it? How much is the rent? What kind of machinery do they use and how much of it? Etc. All of these questions – and answers – will help you predict and plan for your operating budget and possible investment needs.

Buy each of their products and services and dissect them until you have discovered their pros and cons, what makes them tick and how you can make your product or service offering even better.

This is what big corporations do all the time. They benchmark off their competition. You see this with cellular providers. One will come out with a promotion and the other companies follow suit almost immediately.

Why do they follow suit? Simple, to keep and increase market share. It also makes sense that you look to see what you can offer to make a better product or service than your competitor.

It is absolutely critical to know the trends of the industry you are looking to be apart of. This will give you a very clear picture of what the market can bear and how you will "fit" into it in relation to the competition or whether you should enter the market at all.

Let's say you are going to start your own janitorial service. Without spying on the competition, you can't really get a grasp of how many other providers are out there, what services they offer, the prices they demand for those services, the machinery, equipment and vans they need, number of employees, etc.

While "spying," you may even discover ways to set yourself apart. Perhaps you can offer services they don't, or bundle services, or service an audience that is underserved, like apartment complexes or the local community college, etc.

If you don't dig deep to understand what your competition is doing, you'll never know what opportunities exist for you and your own company as well.

Gut Check Time
Questions for Review

- Are you comfortable with spying on your competition?

- Do you now realize the benefits of learning as much as you can about those who might compete against you?

- What would a competitor see if they spied on you?

The Dangers of Expanding Too Fast

Speed is useful only if you are running in the right direction.

—Joel Barker, Future Edge

It may sound counterintuitive but there is a big danger in growing *too* fast in your business.

The fact is, too much growth, too soon, can be as bad – or even worse – than too little growth.

Many businesses truly had a shot at true success but expanded too quickly for their own good and, as a result, lost everything because they were not ready for that growth. It is important to make the right move at the right time. We do not plan for marriage and children at the age of 10? Obviously, that's way too early and could be counterproductive. Same holds true for business. You must evaluate the right timing for expansion. Please remember (Reckless)Speed kills!

I always think about my favorite Chinese restaurant in New York City. It was such a tiny restaurant and they always had a line waiting for their tables. I always wondered why they didn't just move to a bigger place. I now understand why. They knew that the customer base they had supported the restaurant size they were in; period. Moving into a larger space and incurring larger costs would not necessarily bring in more customers. Instead, it would merely drive the costs up and their profits down.

Rather than following their simple strategy for measured growth, I expanded my business too fast and I know that was one of the main keys that lead to its failure. But I told myself the only way to grow my business was to increase my retail placement around the country. This was not true, for us and many who are considering expansion.

Expansion can work, but it must be carefully thought out. You need to make sure you have saturated your local area of opportunity before you move on to greener pastures. Before you expand, first your business should be known as a responsible, trusted and proven brand. You should be turning a profit in your local market before thinking you'll start to make a profit with more stores/outlets. If your business cannot pass this test, then it is simply not the time to take your business to another area and expand. Instead, it is time to find out why your local market is not biting first and apply those lessons to grow where you are before taking those same problems somewhere else!

When you consider expanding your business follow these steps:

- **Have honest conversations with yourself and your team.** Talk about what you're good at, what might be holding you back and ask the following questions before even considering expansion:

  - What feedback are we receiving from our customer base?
  - Why are they not buying more?
  - Are our costs to high?
  - Do people want what we are offering?

- **You want to be a local celebrity where your business is located.** They need to know who you are and be purchasing your products and services on a regular basis. If this is not happening, you need to make some changes until your brand is proven and recognizable. That way, you won't be "starting from scratch" each time you open a new store somewhere else.

- **Create a system.** Finally, make sure that your first business is operating in a way that is repeatable, transferable and successful. Identify the various "systems" in your business – customer service, finances, production, delivery, packaging, etc. – and create a template you can follow in other stores so that those systems can be repeated easily. If a system isn't successful, don't expand until it is!

When you expand into a new location your business profits should support the expansion. If you are going to have to go into personal funds to expand, you need to stop, stop, STOP immediately! This could be a big sign you are going in the wrong direction.

Gut Check Time
Questions for Review

- Have you seriously considered the question of your company's growth?

- Have you had honest conversations about growth between you and your team?

- Do you have a system for how to expand your growth?

- Is there a company you know, perhaps locally, who has grown and expanded in a way you might emulate?

Challenges Provide Opportunities

Everything negative – pressure, challenges – is all an opportunity for me to rise.

—Kobe Bryant

For whatever reason, challenges are not viewed quite as they should be. While many will perceive them as setbacks or obstacles, challenges are actually unrealized opportunities.

When you are faced with a challenge you didn't expect or don't know how to handle, it can provide the opening to tap into potential you did not even know was possible.

Some of my greatest discoveries came out of what most people would consider a major problem, even a crisis, at various times in my life.

Rather than be crushed under the weight of challenges, I took another approach of seeing every challenge as an opportunity and, in fact, some of my greatest strides in life and business have come through this philosophy.

Case in point: When we first started our food line, we were going to prepare frozen entries that included meat in our meal selections. The kitchen we were getting licensed to, however, was only FDA certified. So we could not prepare any products that contained meat. This meant that we had to revamp all of our recipes to be meatless or find a new location. At first, this seemed like a crisis and major stumbling block. In the end, however, that was the niche that gave us the ability to sit at the table with major retailers, something I believe might not have happened if we had simply used meat in our recipes. When faced with challenges, obstacles that look like a crisis, retrain your mind to see it as an opportunity, an advantage or even a complete game changer. Not only will this attitude, or habit, make you less afraid of challenges, it will also open you up to new opportunities even when things look bleak!

Gut Check Time
Questions for Review

- What challenges sprung to mind when we started this chapter?

- How have challenges shaped you in the past?

- What lessons have you learned?

- How do you think those lessons could be applied to starting, closing or growing a business?

Partnerships

The best partnerships aren't dependent on a mere common goal but on a shared path of equality, desire, and no small amount of passion.

—Sarah MacLean

Before you start your company, you need to do an assessment. Ask yourself, what skills do you and your current team possess to make your business successful? I discussed in Chapter 4 what components go into forming a business. Below is a short list of tasks that need to be addressed in your company formation.

- Forming a corporation;

- Trademark;

- Corporate identity;

- Product development;

- Website and online marketing Human Resource;

- Bookkeeping;

- Insurance;

- Legal;

- Marketing;

- Sales;

- Business management;

- Etc.

As you can see, in the list above nothing is really specific to your product or service yet each one is vital to your ultimate success.

> Most people only think about the core business that they want to create. They don't stop to think about all the other aspects that it will take to make their business successful.

It's only natural that we should play to our strengths and focus on what we're passionate about. Not everyone has a degree in business, so I am not faulting anyone who does not understand that all these aspects are needed. And yet… they are needed! It is important that you have these services in place even if your own skill set does not include them. These services can cost a lot and corporations have entire teams focusing on each of those tasks I listed above.

Obviously, you won't be able to do this when you're just starting out, but you *can* find people who possess a lot of these skills, especially if they have MBA's with a business development focus. It can cost a lot of money to have a person like this on your team. How much? Consultants in this area can charge $175 – or more – per hour. Anyone running a business can tell you that it takes hundreds of hours to get it off the ground. So this amount can add up – quickly.

The Power of Partnerships

To defray these costs many start ups look for strategic partners that will fill in the missing gaps in exchange for ownership in their company.

You might know of people who possess these qualities, but if not, look for business consultants. This is what they do for a living. Understand that partners who get in on the early stage of your company get a higher percentage of its earnings than when your business is already a success. Why you may ask is this the case? It all comes down to risk/payout. The one who takes a chance on your entity before there is any clear evidence that the business venture is going to succeed is taking a lot of risk. When your company has proven success less risk is involved so less ownership is given because there will definitely be a payout.

If you find someone that possesses all the criteria you need to move your business ahead, you have to make some decisions. Ask yourself some questions:

- What is their cost?

- Can I afford their cost over time?

- For how long will I need their input?

- Is it worth trading a percentage of my company for their services?

Most likely these are ongoing assignments you are looking for assistance with, and not just a one-time project. If you can't afford the service requested, you aren't necessarily dead in the water, but you are going to need to enter the world of partnerships.

In previous chapters, I said "trust no one". Well, just because you find a partner, that rule doesn't just go out of the window. Instead, it becomes fully loaded. Do your homework and make sure any potential business partner is fully vetted with references and, if possible, a background check.

Once you find a suitable partner, you have to assess what they bring to the table. Usually it is going to be skills or financial resources. We can't be good at everything, but once you've identified a need you can't fill yourself or with current staff members, you are either going to have to hire someone for a traditional salary or, in lieu of salary, provide ownership in exchange for their expertise and/or resources. Before deciding whether to pay someone a salary or offer them partnership, consider how much value they're likely to add to the company. It can be tempting to just "hand off" responsibility to a partner, but do you really need them to do things you can do yourself? Or are their long-term contributions so valuable that it is worthwhile enough to bring them on your team as more than a freelance vendor or part-time employee? There are many options to consider before choosing a partner.

Remember, you don't want to give ownership away when it doesn't make sense and they are not going to significantly move you forward. At the same time, when you do find the right partner, secure them because their impact will be significant.

Consider how a strict percentage partner can impact the business. Let's say you have a great business model, but simply can't get noticed in a crowded marketplace.

You can't afford to pay a full-time social media manager $100,000 a year, but you can afford to offer them, say, 10% of the company's net profits and a small stipend for their time. The opportunity for you could be worth millions in the long run, and be well worth the small "cut" they get of those significant profits they helped to create.

Gut Check Time
Questions for Review

- Is your company a good candidate for partnership?

- Have you identified what, adding a partner will bring to your? Are you comfortable with "selling off" shares – or a percentage – of your company for the extra help you need to get your business off the ground?

Lesson 15

Contracts

A verbal contract isn't worth the paper it's written on.

—Samuel Goldwyn

Once you have found a partner you wish to officially "marry," you need to sign the hefty contract. Naturally, this contract has to be drawn up by an attorney. Most people will tell you that you are signing the most important contract of your life. So you need a contract attorney that is really good so that there are no loopholes.

Sounds pretty reasonable, right? Wrong! Be forewarned: you are going to spend a lot of money drafting this contract which, in most cases, is usually designed to partner with an investor. This investor is typically rich or you would not be asking them for money in the first place. Yet despite the investor's money, contract violation is a very real scenario that happens rather often.

Contract Violation

What happens when your partner says you violated the contract and because of this, they are going to sue you for 100% control of your company?

I know what you're thinking? That could never happen. I would never violate a contract. They would never do that.

Unfortunately, you're wrong. This can – and does – happen all the time. Now, let's say you are completely innocent and did not, in fact, violate the contract. Regardless, a lawsuit is a lawsuit. You are going to have to hire an attorney and probably pay a steep charge, because now you are fighting to keep your company that you worked so hard for.

The problem with this example is your opponent is usually richer than you. What does that mean? Well, with all that money they can hold the case up in court because, unlike your attorney, they have theirs on a yearly retainer for *exactly* this kind of scenario. Meanwhile, your attorney is billing you hourly. If you are wealthy in your own right, then maybe, just maybe, you *might* stand a chance. If not, which is probably why you got the investor in the first place, then you are going to lose even when you are right.

So, how do you avoid this all too common predicament? Well, most people will tell you to get the best attorney you can to draft the initial contract when, in the end, you won't have the resources to defend it.

Instead, I advise you get a good attorney that is reasonable to draw up the agreement, but don't spend thousands of dollars to get it done.

Why? Simple, if your contract is contested, your money you spend drafting the contract will pretty much go down the drain anyway.

What you're trying to do with a reasonably priced lawyer in the first place is to draw up a contract that will work for 95% of the cases.

Almost no contract can stand up to an investor who is really just using the contract violation charge to win a company from their business partner who doesn't have enough money to fight them in court. It is used as frequent strategy more often then not to obtain companies with great potential for a cheap price. It is not right, but business can become very ugly at times.

Gut Check Time
Questions for Review

- Have you ever drawn up a contract before?

- Do you know any good attorneys that have experience in contract law?

- Does anyone you trust know any good attorneys?

Know When To Hold Them, Know When To Fold Them

Hold or Fold is a million dollar question.
Fold before you bleed too much.

—B.S. Rao

Knowing when to keep pursuing a business or when to shut the doors has always been a tough process. Unfortunately, the decision is often made *for* us, instead of by us.

In other words, the idea to shut your doors usually comes when you have run out of money to keep your business going. The important question to ask yourself is "why":

- Where is the money going?

- Are you making profits?

- Are your customers happy?

- Are you busy and growing?

- Then why do you need money?

If your business is turning a profit *and* growing, you should only need money to keep up with growth, not operating costs.

> If you find that you are constantly running out of money and you are also still trying to get your product or service to pick up traction, then you need to gut check yourself.

This is especially true if you are considering tapping into your retirement accounts or emergency funds. If that is the case, I will tell you to **Stop Immediately!** In my case, I needed money for my business to show that it was worth having legs. I had no formal plan for growth, just a vision of what I told myself to be true. Which was that I had a product that people wanted.

So, given that vision, I needed to leverage all personal assets to make my vision come true, right? Wrong, wrong, wrong!

In rushing ahead, I forgot to ask some fairly critical growth questions, such as:

- What happens if the market just doesn't care for my product?

- What if I run into costs I simply didn't, and couldn't, anticipate?

- What happens when I need more money and I tapped out all my resources and personal credit to the point that I have bad credit?

- Where do you go then?

It is at this point where you start getting desperate. I call it "Digging in your mom's purse: syndrome". I will tell you that, living it firsthand, it is an awful place to be. You know things are not going in the right direction, but you just can't get a grip on how to turn them around. You keep telling yourself to hold on for the miracle.

While you wait, you take your light bill money, rent/mortgage money, car payment, and even your food money to keep the company afloat, waiting for that magical moment that may not ever come.

It starts a painful cycle that, unfortunately, usually leads to business closure. It does *not* have to end this way, if only you'll be observant, stay calm and watch for signs along the way. Speaking of, there were *clear* signs along the way that

I missed. I believed so much in what I was doing to a fault, ignoring the signs. I wanted to believe it would happen for me despite the red flags.

What I learned – and want *you* to learn – is make a "high" *and* a "low" exit strategy:

The High Exit Strategy

A high exit strategy details how you want to exit your business if it is profitable and successful. In other words, you have grown your business to the high end of the scale and want to leave it strategically.

For example, the answer could be "I want to sell it for a profit" or "I want to pass the business down to my children," etc.

Either way, you want to plan for how you plan to exit when your business is successful.

The Low Exit Strategy

The low exit strategy is when your business is not performing for an extended period of time and you have reached your planned capital investment level.

At this point, you will have to decide to either dissolve the business or sell it to keep it going and turn things around. This is a tough decision and a crucial one. Staying with a business too long without a profit puts you at risk for losing everything, while shutting it down before things turn around can crush your spirit.

It is important to note that just because you have to dissolve your business does not mean you are a failure. At that point, you have learned so much valuable information that it actually might be the launch pad to what you are truly supposed to do – just with another company or opportunity altogether. Many entrepreneurs whose successes we admire only went on to succeed after they'd failed at one or more earlier business opportunities.

In the famous words of Walt Disney himself, "I think it's important to have a good hard failure when you're young. I learned a lot out of that. Because it makes you aware of what can happen to you. Because of it I've never had any fear in my whole life when we've been near collapse. I've never been afraid or had the feeling I couldn't walk out and get a job doing something."

The biggest take away is, do not keep funding a losing business. A losing business is one that is not making more money than it costs to run the business. In simpler terms, if your business brings in $20 in "profit," but it costs $40 to run it, it is time to have the tough conversation. Gut check time, as it's known.

Gut Check Time
Questions for Review

- Have you considered your own exit strategy?

- Will you be able to put your emotions on the back burner if it's clear the company is failing?

How You Close Defines Success or Failure

Failure after long perseverance is much grander than never to have a striving good enough to be called a failure.

—George Eliot

How you close your business is just as important as how you start your business. It's a lot like dating. It's always easier to break up with someone when there is another on the horizon. The same applies in business.

You should not be closing your business without a plan.

If you are going to leverage the business that did not work to open another one, you need to leverage and pull all the assets you can out of your old business. I do not mean the physical equipment, although you might need that as well. I am talking about the lessons, trials, mistakes, challenges, success and relationships that were formed in the process. They will all contribute to your future success, even if they didn't culminate in success the first time around.

Do not burn bridges along the way. One of the hardest things to do is to go back to the people that believed in you and your ideas and say to them, "Thank you for the opportunity, but I am closing my business." However, it's the only way to keep that relationship honest, open and respectful. You have to respect the other person enough to swallow your pride and confess your failure.

You have to swallow your pride, but it shows a level of maturity that many others lack. I am speaking first hand.

You never know how much that relationship will be needed in the future, personally and/or professionally, so whatever you do, don't burn your bridges on the way up, or down, your entrepreneurial ladder.

Gut Check Time
Questions for Review

- Do you have a plan for closing – or transitioning – your business?

- Do you recognize the power of closing a business properly – and well – to leave doors open for the future?

- Do you understand the power of failure and how it can often return as the "prize" of knowledge in moving forward with a new, often better, opportunity?

Conclusion

You Are What You Think

Finally, please take this message along with you: **you are what you think**. Think positively, and you will act positively. Think negatively, and you will act negatively.

You are a product of what you think. It is so important to focus on what you want and the direction you want your business to go in and never think about anything different.

Make all your decisions with that intention. If you waiver in your heart, then you will make decisions that reflect that thought. If you are afraid that no one will want your product or service, then your subconscious decisions will reflect being afraid versus confidence that you have a product or service that the public wants and needs.

These thoughts manifest themselves in your actions. Your mind produces the thoughts and your actions reinforce them, so the more positive your thoughts, the more positive your actions.

What you think in your mind puts out subconscious messages in the way you communicate your ideas, products or services to the world.

Of course, there is always a level of uncertainty when you embark on something unfamiliar. **One thing I am sure of in life is that there are no mistakes.**

You are doing what you are doing at the right time and each experience will be placed in your toolbox for current and future use so nothing is a waste. It is simply wisdom.

There will be naysayers in your path, folks will tell you to ignore your vision, but that is because this vision was given to you, not to them. I had naysayers around me who seemed to inevitably get on board when the destination was no longer an option. When success was still an option, they would point out all the faults in my plan. When they sensed failure in the air, they were the first to say, "Told you so!" or you should not quit because you invested so much of your time. Which leads me to another point: surround yourself with like-minded people. I know I have mentioned this concept several times in the book, but you are who you hang around with. I do not mean people who agree with all the same things you do, but people who are going after their purpose and utilize their instincts to make decisions. People who are entrepreneurs like yourself.

It is hard to get someone who is an employee to understand how you think, because most times they are thinking through their 9 to 5 glasses. There is nothing wrong with that, just understand that means they are not thinking about the 9,000 other components that an entrepreneur has to think about and manage. Entrepreneurs have to focus on all the variables that make a business run effectively.

It takes other visionaries to truly understand and provide proper insight to assist you with where you are going. Of course, this is not an absolute statement. I am saying that surrounding yourself with like minded people will help propel your business in the right direction.

THE UNTOLD TRUTH ABOUT BUILDING A STARTUP

Gut Check Time
Questions for Review

- Who are you surrounding yourself with?

- Are they like-minded people or "Debbie Downers"?

- Are they positive, uplifting, and wise or negative and defeating?

Your answer to those questions will often determine your success, because who you hang around with affects how you think, and how you think determines how – and if – you succeed.

About the Author

From concept to production, Jilea Hemmings has a distinct affinity for branding and product development. As founder and CEO of Eshe Consulting, she aids small and medium companies in all aspects of their business. From assisting in the business and product development stages for start-up companies to helping existing companies rebrand their product and overall image, Eshe Consulting truly does it all. Her past role as founder and operator of Greenie Tots afforded a unique insight and invaluable opportunity to further hone her skills as a talented entrepreneur and small business specialist. As the first frozen all natural meatless entrée line for kids, Greenie Tots appeared on the shelves of major retailers across the United States. Some of her most recent accomplishments include being named by Legacy Magazine as one of South Florida's 25 Most Influential & Prominent Black Women in Business (2012), as well as being awarded with the Entrepreneur Product of the Year (2013) and Media Pitch Winner (2013). In addition to her wide range of professional experience, Jilea also received her MBA from Florida Agricultural & Mechanical University. She currently resides in South Florida with her husband and three children and is a passionate advocate for Autism awareness.

www.ingramcontent.com/pod-product-compliance
Lightning Source LLC
Chambersburg PA
CBHW071214200326
41519CB00018B/5512